GROOVE STUDIES

Accents and Ghost Notes: The Subtleties of Great Drumming

by Adam Moses

Edited by Rick Mattingly

Cover Sketch: Melissa Griffith

ISBN 978-1-61780-716-9

7777 W. BLUEMOUND RD. P.O. BOX 13819 MILWAUKEE, WI 53213

In Australia Contact:
Hal Leonard Australia Pty. Ltd.
4 Lentara Court
Cheltenham, Victoria, 3192 Australia
Email: ausadmin@halleonard.com.au

Visit Hal Leonard Online at
www.halleonard.com

CONTENTS

INTRODUCTION

Throughout my years of teaching, I've noticed a trend with many intermediate students. They are usually quick to develop the coordination required to play different types of beats, but they often sound stiff or robotic. Many beginning drummers dedicate their time behind the kit trying to play as many different rhythms as fast as they can without stopping to think about the subtleties that make a beat really groove. They often exert a lot of energy by playing with tense muscles due to poor technique and execution. They then begin to lose faith in their ability because what they are playing doesn't sound like the recording they are trying to emulate. More often than not, they tend to play at one volume level and don't stop to notice the nuances that make their favorite drummers sound so good. Being a great drummer doesn't happen overnight, and shortcutting the time it takes to develop good technique and feel results in having a slightly larger vocabulary of mediocre-sounding beats.

All of the reputable drummers have spent hours upon hours honing their skills to the point that they don't have to think about what they are doing; they just play. It is not enough to simply work through these exercises. When you get to the point of "not having to think about it" and feel comfortable while playing, this is when you will be able to make it sound great.

Slowing the beats/patterns down and focusing on the components that really make them groove is the only way to fully understand and perfect the note placement within a rhythm.

Being able to play a fast or complex rhythm is pointless if it doesn't have a good feel. This book is aimed at intermediate-level players to help them focus on applying the skills and concepts they have already learned. We are now going to start to inject your drumming with life, character, and feel. I have written these exercises to be a study in timing, motion, coordination, technique, and touch, coupled with exercises that are fun and useful.

The key to a good groove is steady time (read: practicing with a metronome) and the use of *dynamics*— i.e., mixing loud and soft strokes, accents, and ghost notes, etc. In this book, we'll look at the various components necessary to achieve this with specific exercises and examples.

Becoming a proficient musician of any kind requires *listening* to the style of music you wish to play. I can't stress the point of listening enough. There is no substitute for playing along with recordings; this is how you will develop "feel." Learning the coordination from a book is only a part of musical education. You must listen, listen, listen.

The eighth-note *ostinato* (a rhythm that repeats itself) is to be played on the hi-hat over varying snare drum accents and ghost notes. In the advanced section, there are several more hi-hat or ride cymbal ostinatos that can be used in place of the eighth-note hi-hat ostinatos. As they require significantly more coordination and independence, you should only begin working on these after the other chapters have been mastered. Doing otherwise will no doubt become an exercise in frustration.

Happy Drumming!

ABOUT THE AUTHOR

Adam Moses began banging on a child's drumset at age 3 and destroyed them within a month. He adamantly took over his father's 1980 Gretsch set, which was later gifted to him upon high school graduation. After excelling in Kindermusic, Adam was enrolled in classical piano lessons at age 7 and played drums for church services throughout his teen years. At age 15, Adam started taking drum lessons in order to advance his technique. Since then, he has played with numerous bands and renowned artists across a variety of genres. In 2009, Adam assembled and is currently the manager of his variety band, Empty Pocket. He also teaches drum lessons in Greensboro, N.C. and is continuously involved with several bands and various creative projects and recordings.

ACKNOWLEDGMENTS

Thanks to my family—my dad for the drums and inspiration, my mom for never complaining about the noise, and my sister who did complain but always supported and believed in me. I would like to thank Chris Lord for his help with every stage of writing this book. I would also like to thank everyone at Hal Leonard for all the work they have put into making this book happen.

Audio Tracks

Bill Stevens: Recording and mixing

Steve Clarke: Bass

Jim Mayberry: Guitar

Adam Moses: Drums

HOW TO USE THIS BOOK

Each technique exercise should first be practiced at a slow tempo (about 60 bpm) to gain complete control over the techniques and coordination before moving on to a faster tempo. One of the main focuses at the intermediate level of playing is going to be on technique. I suggest raising the tempo by a few bpm at a time after an exercise has been mastered at the slower tempo. Doing this also allows you to keep track of your progress with each exercise.

Once a maximum speed for a particular exercise has been reached—110 bpm, for example—try raising the tempo by 5 bpm (to 115 bpm) and see if you can keep up with the click. If you can't, then back it back down by 3 bpm instead of 5 bpm (to 112 bpm). Once that speed is mastered, up it by another 5 bpm (to 117 bpm). This stair-stepping tempo method should result in being able to play the given exercise faster with the same amount of control.

You should strive to execute the lessons in this book at a variety of tempos and dynamic levels, all with the same amount of control. Never sacrifice control for speed.

Practicing with a metronome is imperative when playing new variations. It allows you to hear the precise placement of the grace notes and the accents against a quarter- or eighth-note pulse. This is where the groove is. You can play around with pushing the beat or pulling it, but this isn't the book for that. An eighth-note pulse on the metronome may be more helpful when first starting the exercises.

Some of the exercises are demonstrated on audio files so you can hear how they are supposed to sound. The demo tracks include each pattern in an exercise, with a couple of seconds of silence in between. There are also some full band tracks so you can hear selected grooves in context. On those tracks, I'm only playing the last pattern in the example.

CHAPTER 1

Basic Beats with Accented Quarter Notes on the Hi-Hat

This chapter is dedicated to developing a rocking motion with the right hand on the hi-hat. The goal is to develop an accent on beats 1, 2, 3, and 4 (the downbeats) followed by unaccented eighth notes in between (the upbeats). The accented quarter notes should be played with the shoulder of the stick on the edge of the hi-hat. The unaccented notes should be played with the tip of the stick on the flat surface of the hi-hat.

Rocking the Wrist

This "wrist rocking" exercise is designed to get the intermediate player used to incorporating accents on the hi-hat. This basic technique is also used to incorporate accents and non-accents with linear styles of playing, but that is for another book. The louder accented notes on the hi-hat give the rhythm that steady pulse that makes you want to bob your head or sway back and fourth. The unaccented notes give the rhythm its body. It's all about putting feeling into drumming, not just being a static timekeeper.

Begin by playing slow quarter notes on the hi-hat using an arm stroke, allowing the wrist to flow with the motion of the arm. Remember to keep your arms and fingers relaxed and loose; this will help with the overall technique and allow for more endurance and a smoother sounding beat. This is the downstroke.

As you are moving your forearm back up to get ready for the next downstroke, drop your wrist so that the tip of the stick lands on the flat surface of the hi-hat. This is the upstroke that produces the unaccented eighth note on the upbeat.

The left foot, or hi-hat foot, should be keeping constant pressure on the hi-hat pedal—not so tightly that the accented note is choked and doesn't sound differently than the non-accented note, and not so loose that it rings for the duration of a quarter note. We're just looking for a good balance between the two extremes.

1

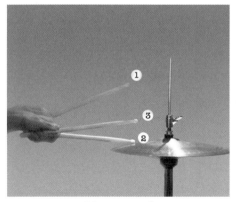
Unaccented

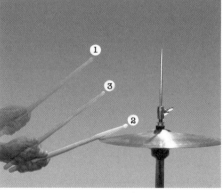
Accented

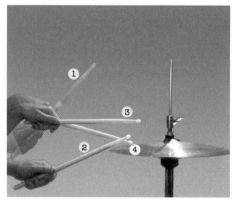
Rocking the Wrist

Practice this on the hi-hat alone until the motion begins to feel comfortable. Then try playing the first beat in this section with this hi-hat technique. The goal is to be able to put the right hand/hi-hat hand on "autopilot" with this technique—to not even have to think about it—while playing variations on the bass drum, much like you have been able to do while playing beats without the accented quarter note.

Though you've probably played the beats in this section many times, it's important to develop this "wrist rocking" technique against the basic beats before moving on to the next chapter, as the exercises will get more confusing if this isn't solid. Each beat should be repeated until you no longer have to think about what the hi-hat hand is doing. This chapter is the foundation on which we will be building more difficult rhythms. As always, the use of a metronome is strongly suggested.

The Rimshot

For the exercises in this chapter, use a rimshot on the snare drum for beats 2 and 4. This will thicken and project the sound of the snare drum. A rimshot is achieved by striking the snare drum head and the rim at the same time. The tip of the stick should strike the center of the head while the shaft of the stick strikes the rim simultaneously. Different effects can be achieved by striking the head in different areas while hitting the rim. The closer the tip strikes to the rim, the more hollow and higher pitched the sound will be.

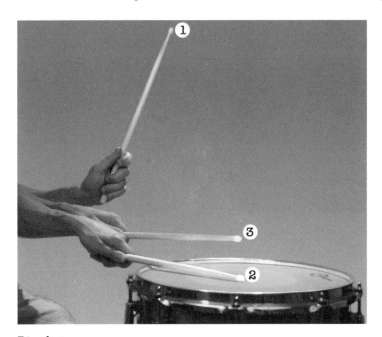

Rimshot

Listen to the audio track for the difference between normal snare hits (measure 1) and rimshots (measure 2).

This technique will also be used in later chapters for accenting purposes. Learning it now will allow for a much easier transition into the next chapter.

Quarter-Note Accented Hi-Hat with Bass Drum Variations

CHAPTER 2

Grooving the Basic Beats

In this chapter, we'll be expanding upon the basic beats from the previous chapter and start filling them up with ghost notes on the snare. The subtle ghost notes contained within this chapter, and those to come, are a component to feeling why a beat grooves. Ghost notes tend to be felt more than heard. The notes you choose to play and the way you play them are important.

Dynamics make a good drummer sound great. Without dynamics, all we are left with is a static beat and, quite often, just noise.

Developing a good meter by playing with a metronome is the mark of a good drummer. If you are overly busy and unable to keep good time, then it's pointless to learn intricate rhythms; the point of these exercises is to develop precision within the quarter note coupled with dynamics.

The exercises from here on are not meant to be used exactly as written in a musical situation. Rather, they are tools to develop the coordination to be able to use any possible sixteenth note for any musical situation and to pick which ones will best complement the music if needed.

The Ghost Note

Ghost notes on the snare drum tend to give a beat more body. A ghost note is an unaccented snare strike that helps to fill out a basic beat and add texture and depth to the rhythm. Ghost notes on the snare should be played one-half- to one-inch above the playing surface. Relaxing the muscles in your arm and hand, and letting the tip of the stick fall close to the center of the snare head is the best way to produce a ghost note. A ghost note doesn't require much force.

Accented notes should be played six to eight inches above the playing surface. Rimshots should be used for the accents.

Basic Beats with Increasing Ghost Notes

The hi-hat and bass drum will play a constant pattern in measures A–E and will only vary with each numbered exercise. The snare drum will be the only variation in measures A–E. Each measure should be repeated as many times as needed until the pattern feels comfortable. By using this method, you can learn the feel of each ghost note against each bass drum pattern before moving on to the more difficult variations.

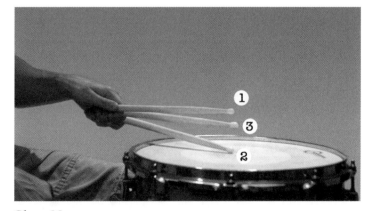

Ghost Note

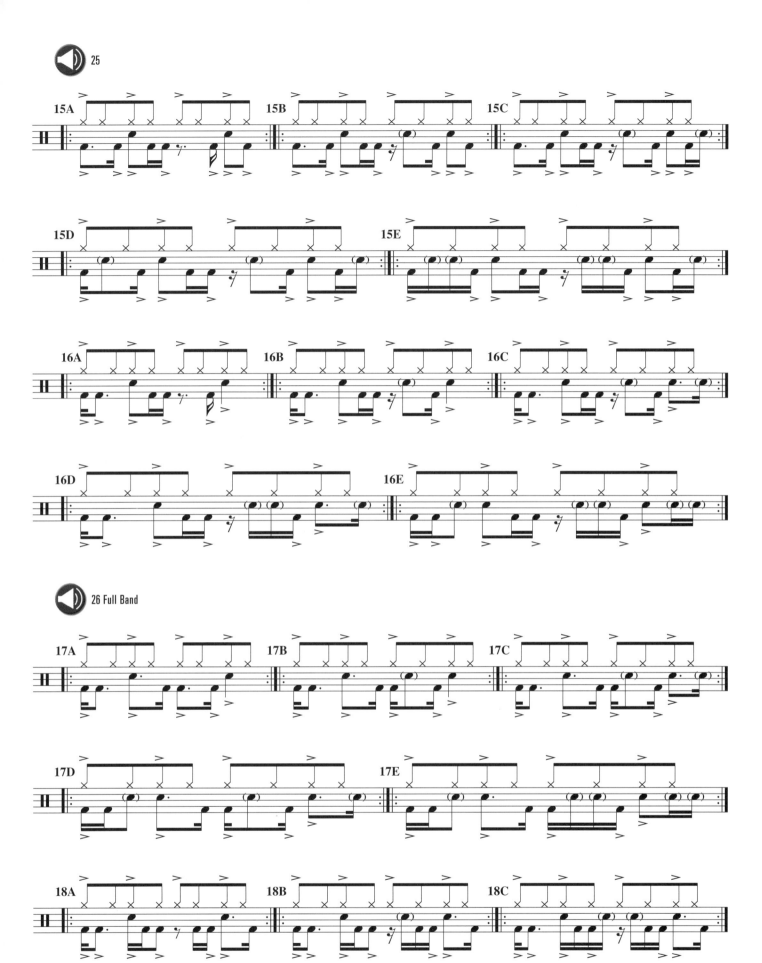

CHAPTER 3

Pull-Outs and Controlled Strokes

Four Strokes

Before getting into pull-outs and controlled strokes on the drumset, we must first discuss four different strokes. The application of these strokes is where the pull-outs and controlled strokes will derive their unique sound. Each is used in accordance with the following stroke of the same hand. Each exercise should be practiced slowly by exaggerating the motion of each stroke; this will allow for maximum understanding of the motion of the strokes, and will make it easier to feel and see the difference of each stroke.

The following accent exercises will help to achieve this technique. The first three exercises will be played with one hand only to help with concentrating on each individual stroke. Once a general concept of the techniques is in place, move on to the single-stroke accent exercises. Make sure that you are not picking the stick up for the upstroke and the tap before striking the head. For the tap, you only need to relax the muscles in your hand with the tip of the stick about an inch away from the head. If you pick the stick up higher before striking the head, it will result in a louder note.

After these strokes have been practiced and applied to the rudiments, you should notice that your rudiments feel more fluid and sound smoother, with crisp accents and even-sounding unaccented notes. A complete understanding of these techniques is necessary to achieve maximum results from the exercises in this book.

Full Stroke: starts high, ends high (accented note)

Downstroke: starts high, ends low (accented note)

Upstroke: starts low, ends high (unaccented note). It will end up looking like the second stroke for the wrist rocking motion on the hi-hat.

Tap: starts low, ends low (unaccented note)

Four-Stroke Exercises

Accent Exercises for the Four Strokes with One Hand

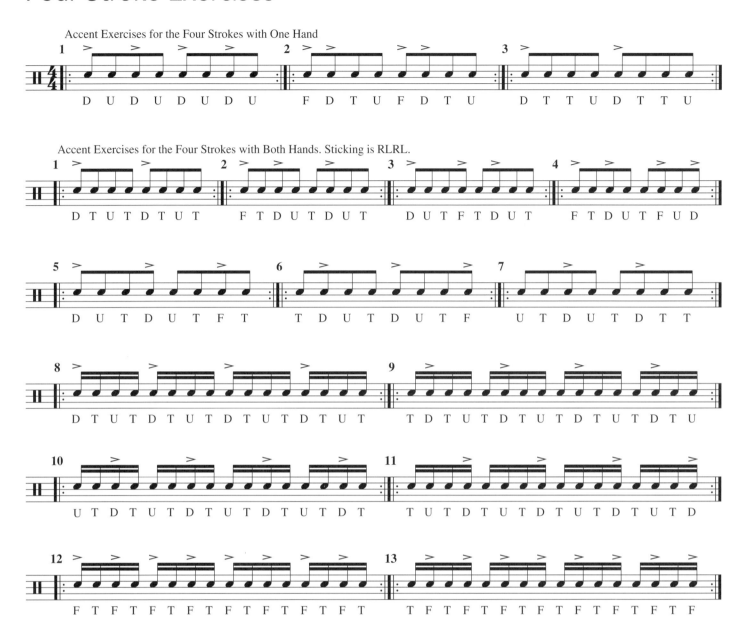

1

D U D U D U D U

2

F D T U F D T U

3

D T T U D T T U

Accent Exercises for the Four Strokes with Both Hands. Sticking is RLRL.

1

D T U T D T U T

2

F T D U T D U T

3

D U T F T D U T

4

F T D U T F U D

5

D U T D U T F T

6

T D U T D U T F

7

U T D U T D T T

8

D T U T D T U T D T U T D T U T

9

T D T U T D T U T D T U T D T U

10

U T D T U T D T U T D T U T D T

11

T U T D T U T D T U T D T U T D

12

F T F T F T F T F T F T F T F T

13

T F T F T F T F T F T F T F T F

The Controlled Stroke

In this section, we begin with utilizing the controlled stroke applied to the drumset. The controlled stroke is an accented note followed by a non-accented note played with the same hand. This will be a downstroke followed by a tap. I have also incorporated the use of a thirty-second-note double stroke, also known as a drag, to be played as ghost notes in these exercises.

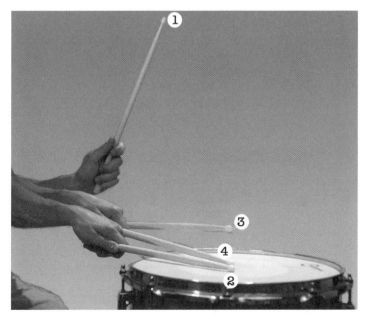

Controlled Stroke

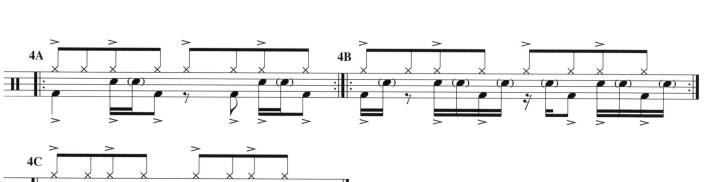

This is the first exercise where a ghost note doubles B.D.

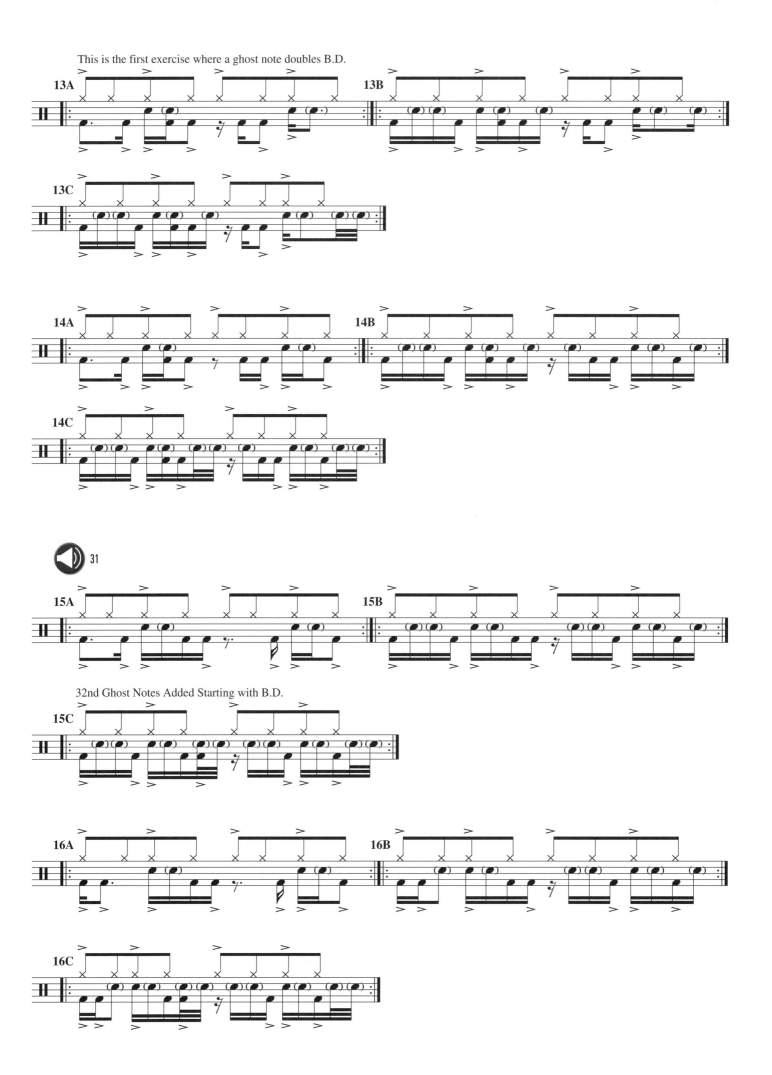

32nd Ghost Notes Added Starting with B.D.

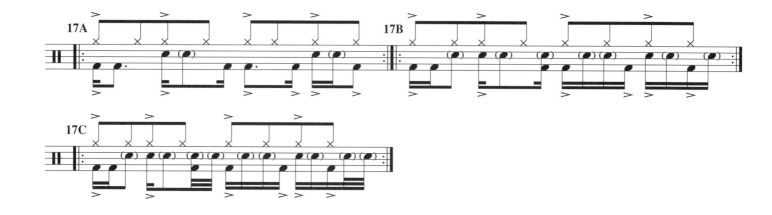

🔊 32 Full Band

The Pull-Out

Pull-Out

The pull-out is an inverted controlled stroke—a non-accented note followed by an accented note played with the same hand. This is achieved by using an upstroke followed by a downstroke. With these exercises, I have started using ghost notes atop of bass drum notes. Using ghost notes in this way really gives the beat a nice thick body.

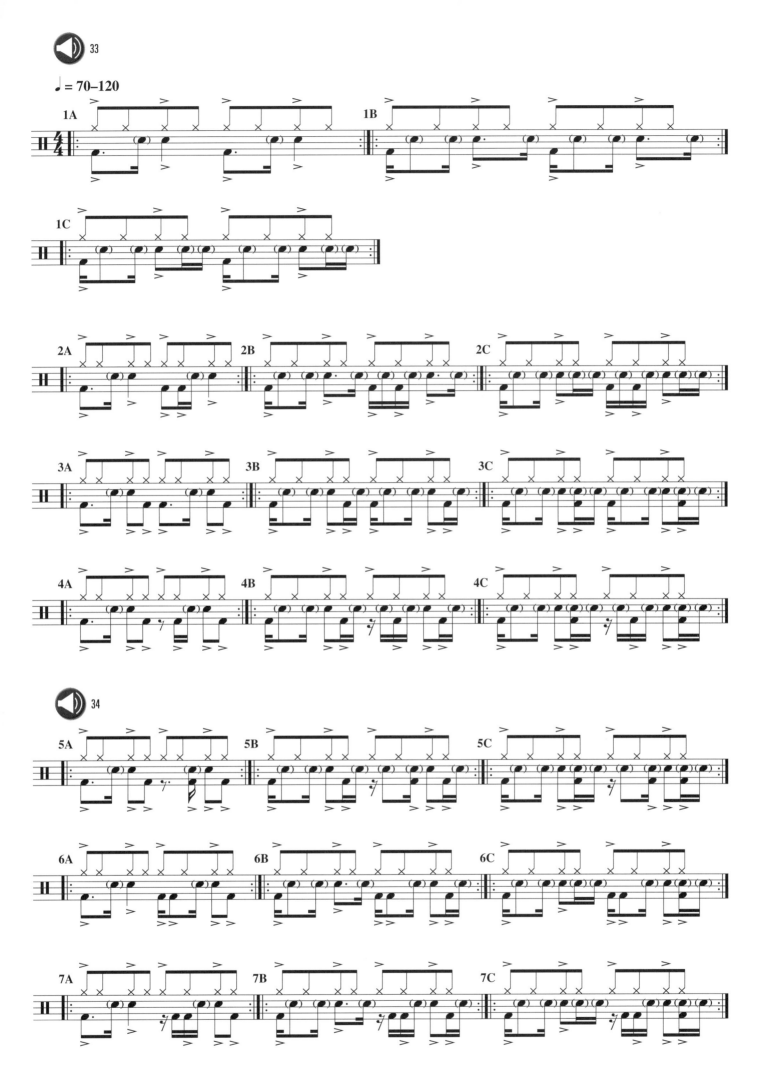

35 Full Band

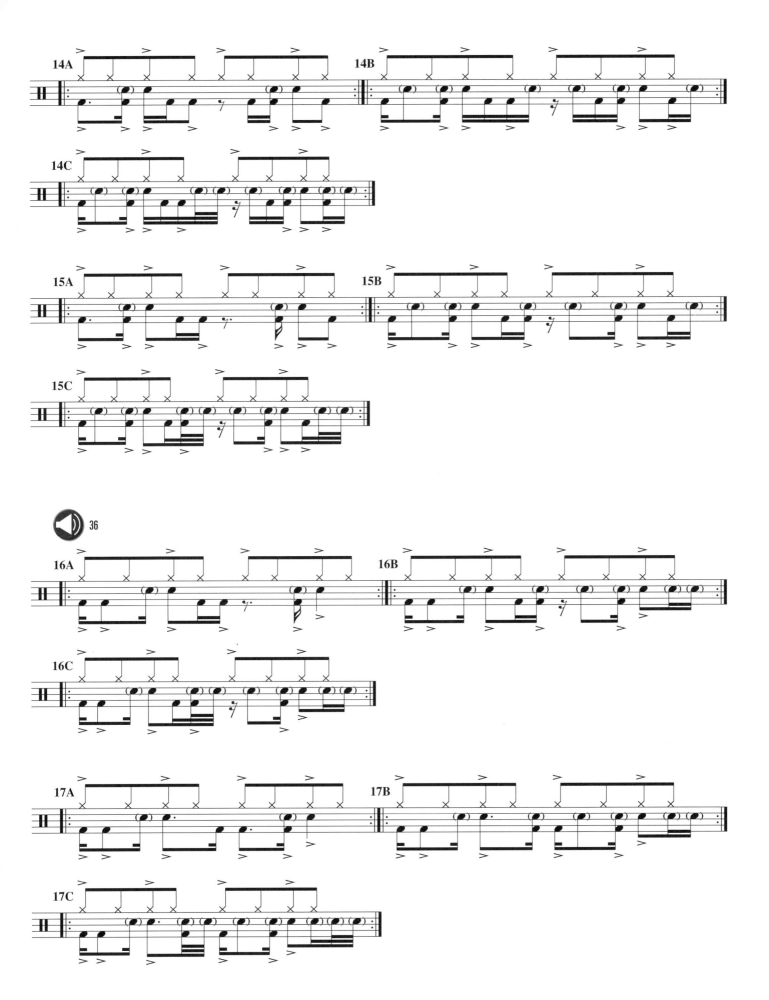

Pull-Outs with Controlled Strokes

This is a ghost note, followed by an accent, followed by a ghost note—an upstroke, a downstroke, and a tap.

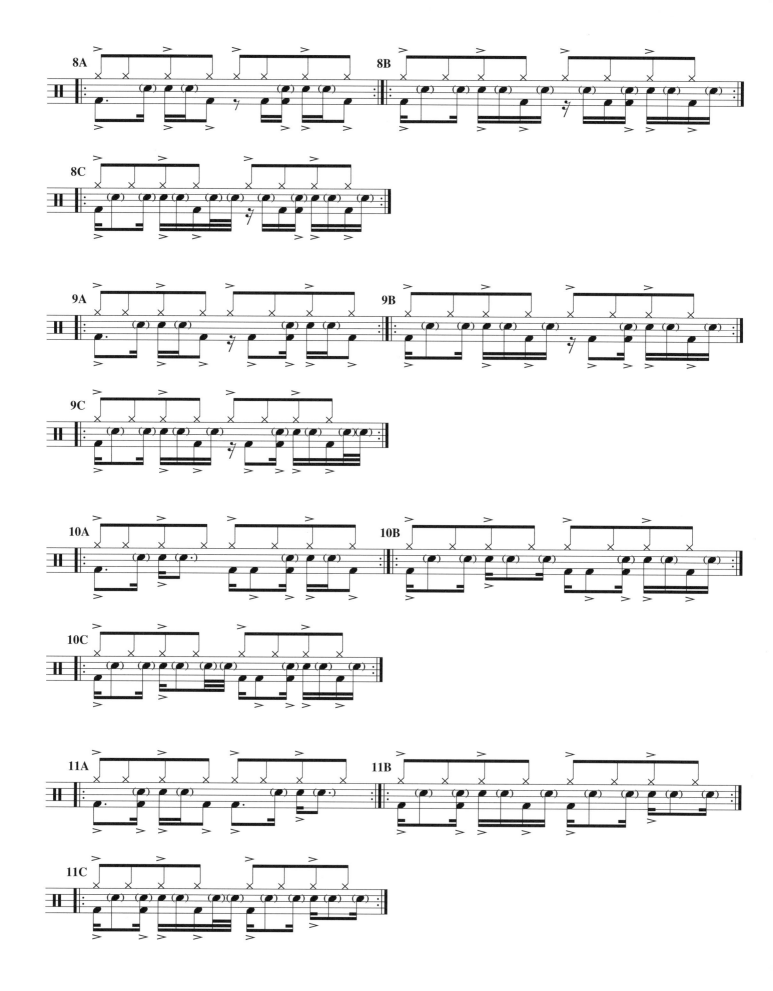

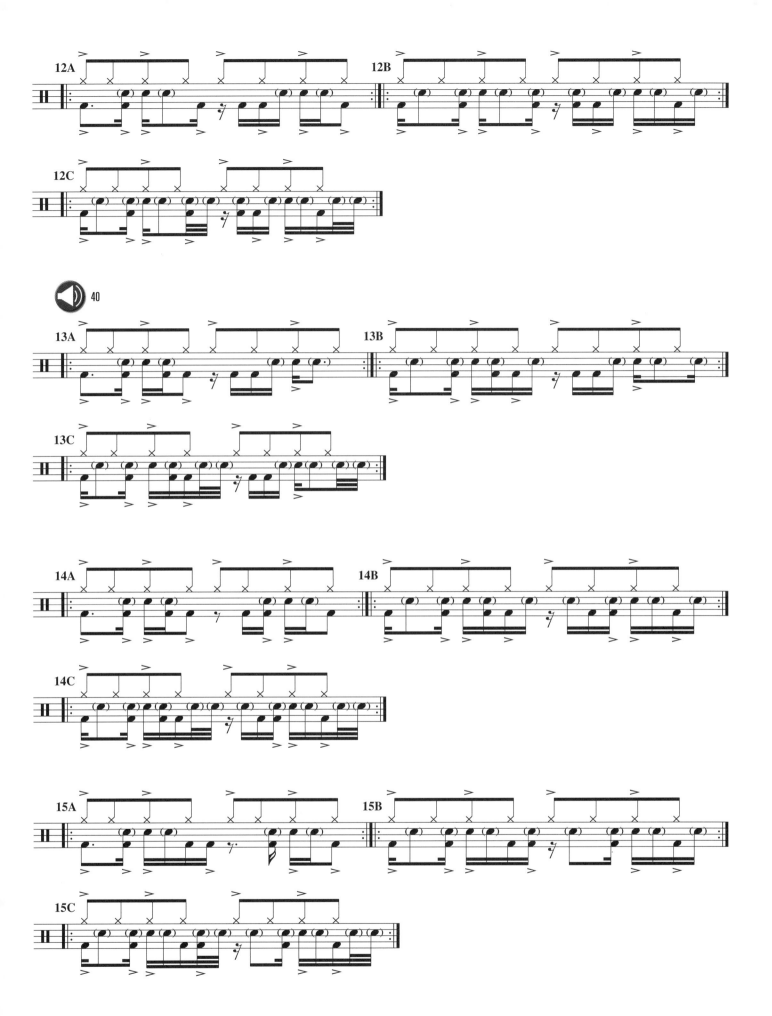

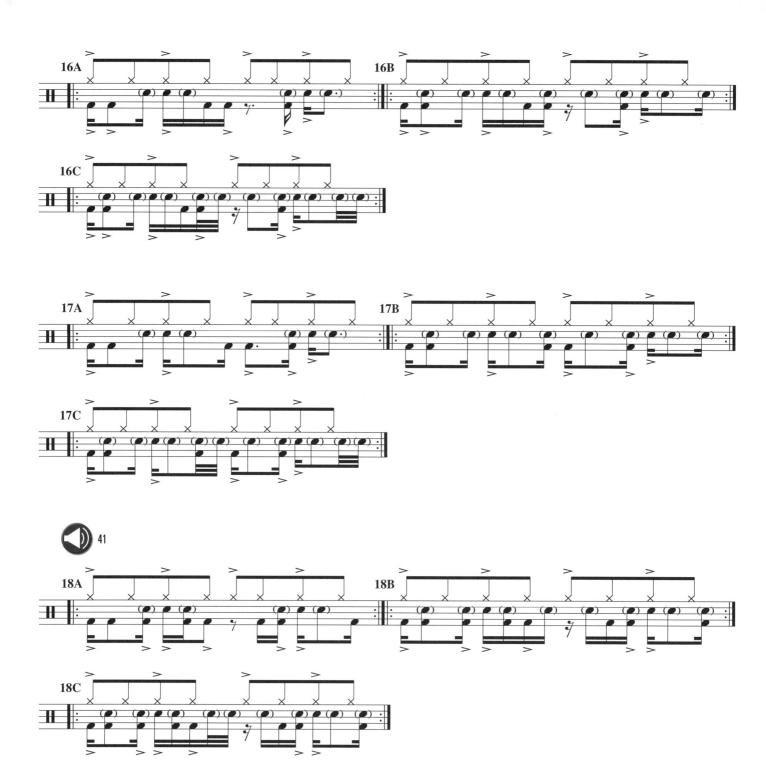

CHAPTER 4

Off-Beat Snare Drum Grooves

While beats 1 and 3 are considered the downbeats, 2 and 4 are considered the "upbeats" or "backbeats." At times, music calls for something different than a 2 and 4 backbeat. You may want to hit the snare drum accent before or after the 2 or 4. This can give the music a different feel altogether, such as Chad Smith's playing in the song "Soul to Squeeze" by Red Hot Chili Peppers. You may also want to place the snare accent with the accent of another instrument. We will first be playing the accent on the "a" of 1, the sixteenth note before beat 2. Here are some exercises to help you hone the feel and technique for this kind of beat.

Off-Beat Snare Drum on the "a" of 1

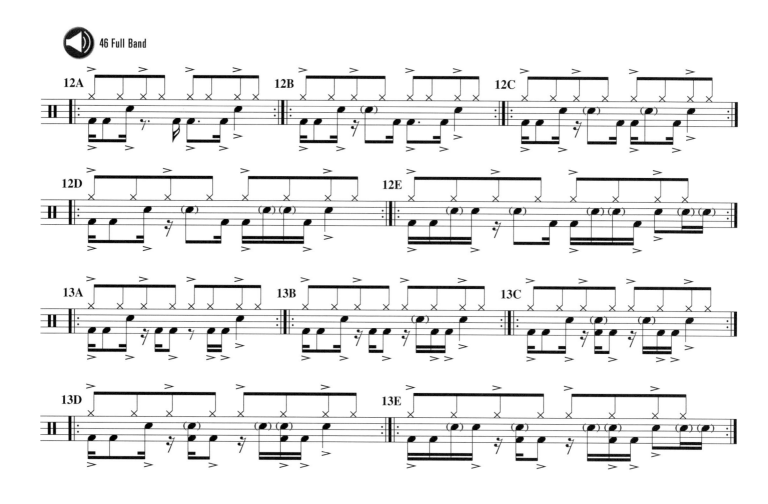

Off-Beat Snare Drum on the "e" of 2

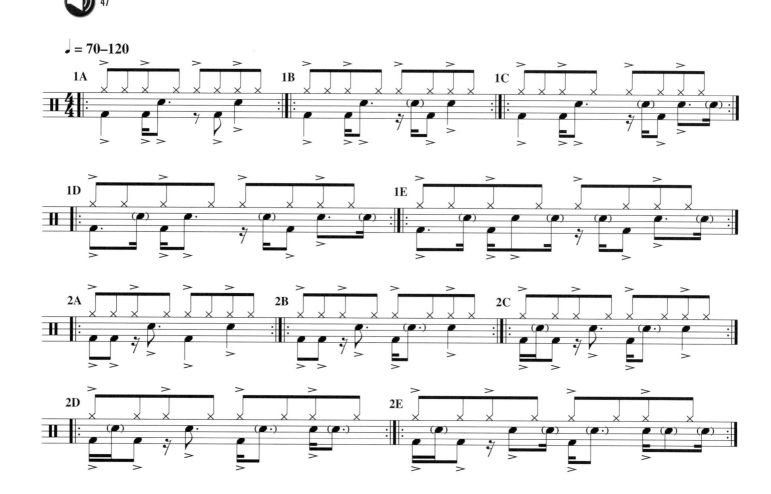

34

Off-Beat Snare Drum on the "&" of 2

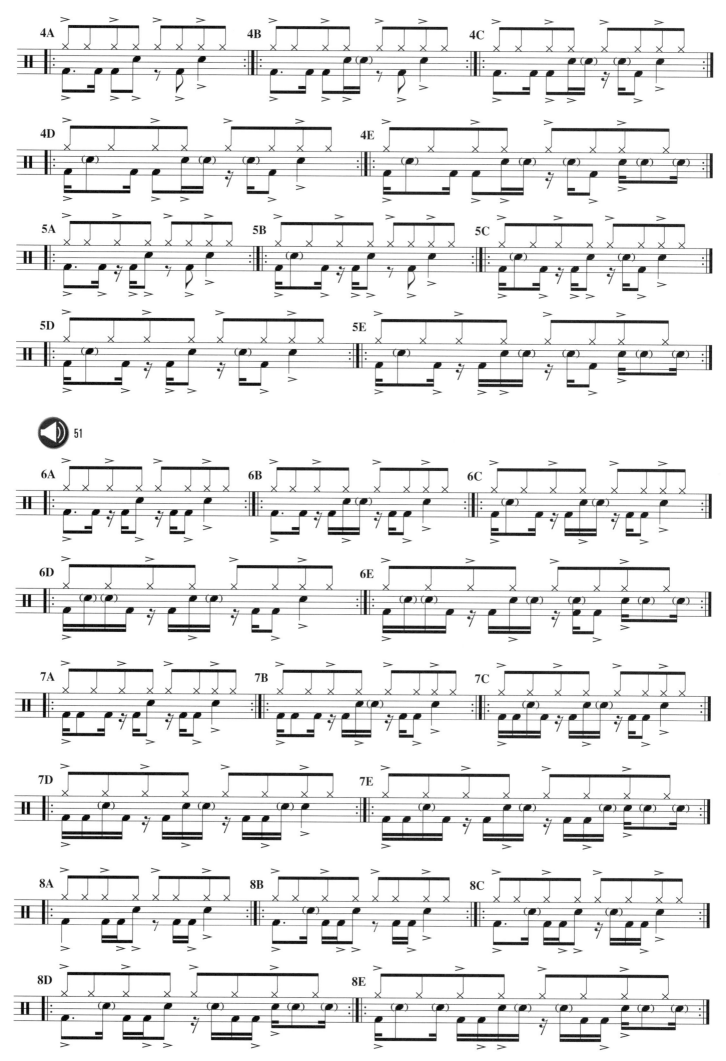

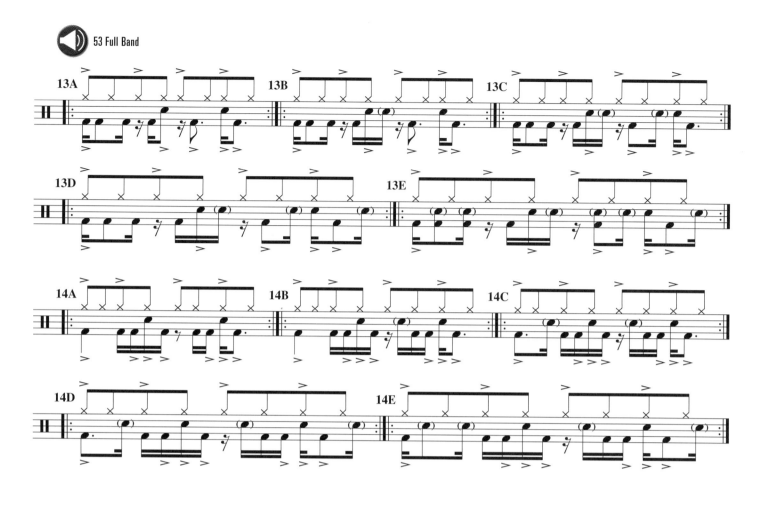

Off-Beat Snare Drum on the "a" of 3

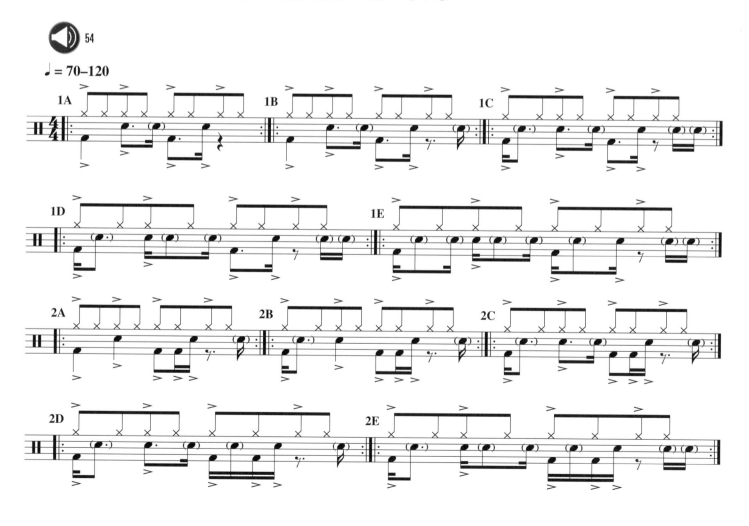

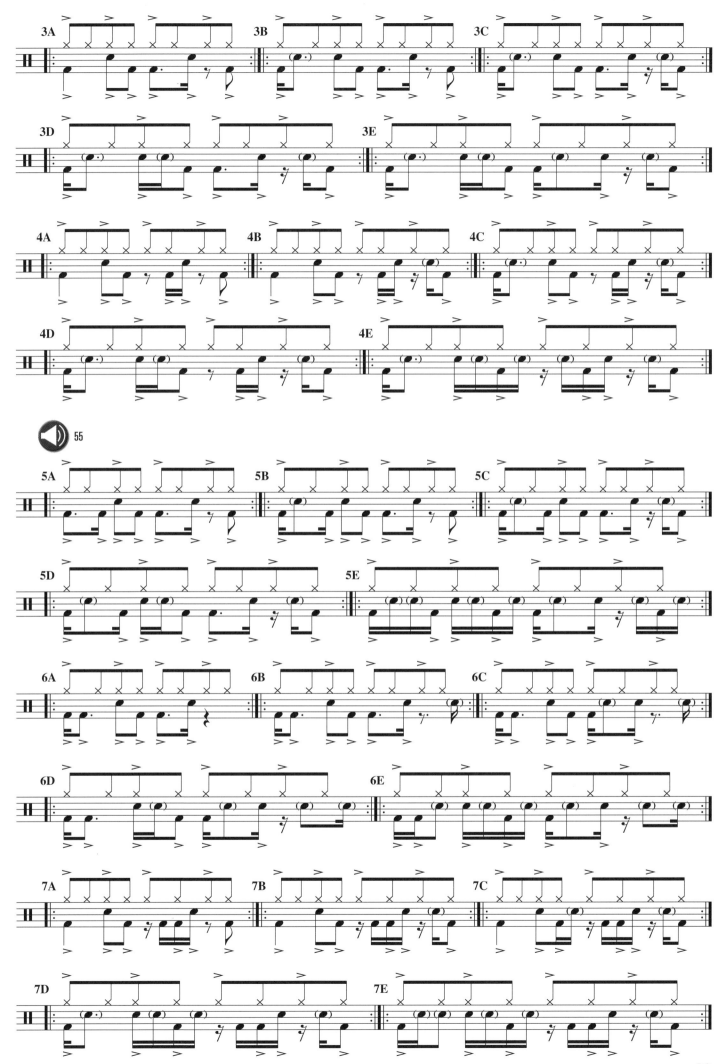

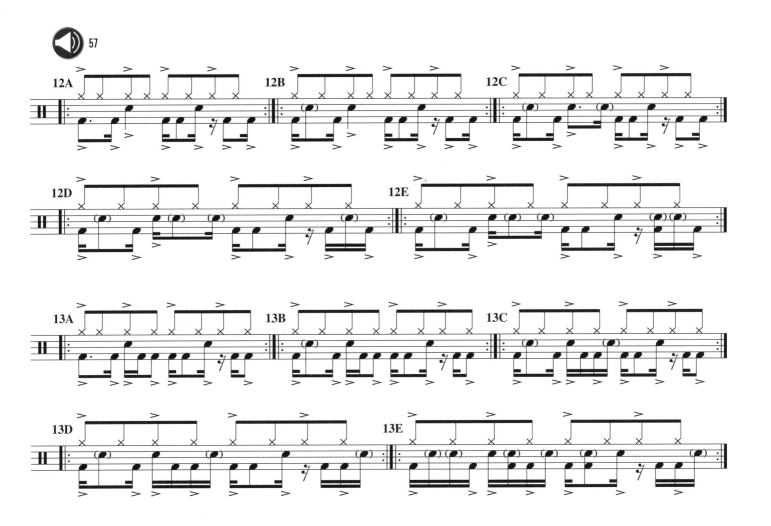

CHAPTER 5

Triplets and Shuffles

It is important to have a good understanding of triplets to develop a good shuffle. They can be played very tight or very loose, as with any beat. The more on top of the quarter note you play, the tighter it will sound.

We will begin by taking a quarter-note hi-hat ostinato and concentrating on the conversation between the snare and bass drum. I believe it is easier to first learn the triplet feel between the snare and bass drum while playing straight quarter notes on the hi-hat, then moving on to the shuffle patterns on the cymbals. This will allow for more concentration on dynamics applied to the snare and bass drum without having to worry about the coordination with a standard shuffle cymbal ostinato. Once a good feel and understanding of this method has been established, we will begin working on adapting the different cymbal ostinatos over the notated beats.

Keep in mind that the exercises in this book are written purely for developing coordination and dynamics, to give you the ability to play what is needed for a given song. More often than not, keeping it simple with tasteful accents will work the best for the majority of musical situations.

Working through these exercises slowly at first will help to develop muscle memory and the ability to put the cymbal ostinato on autopilot while the snare drum and bass drum dance through the measure. Setting your metronome to eighth-note triplets will help with learning the note placement of these shuffle patterns.

Triplets with Quarter-Note Hi-Hat

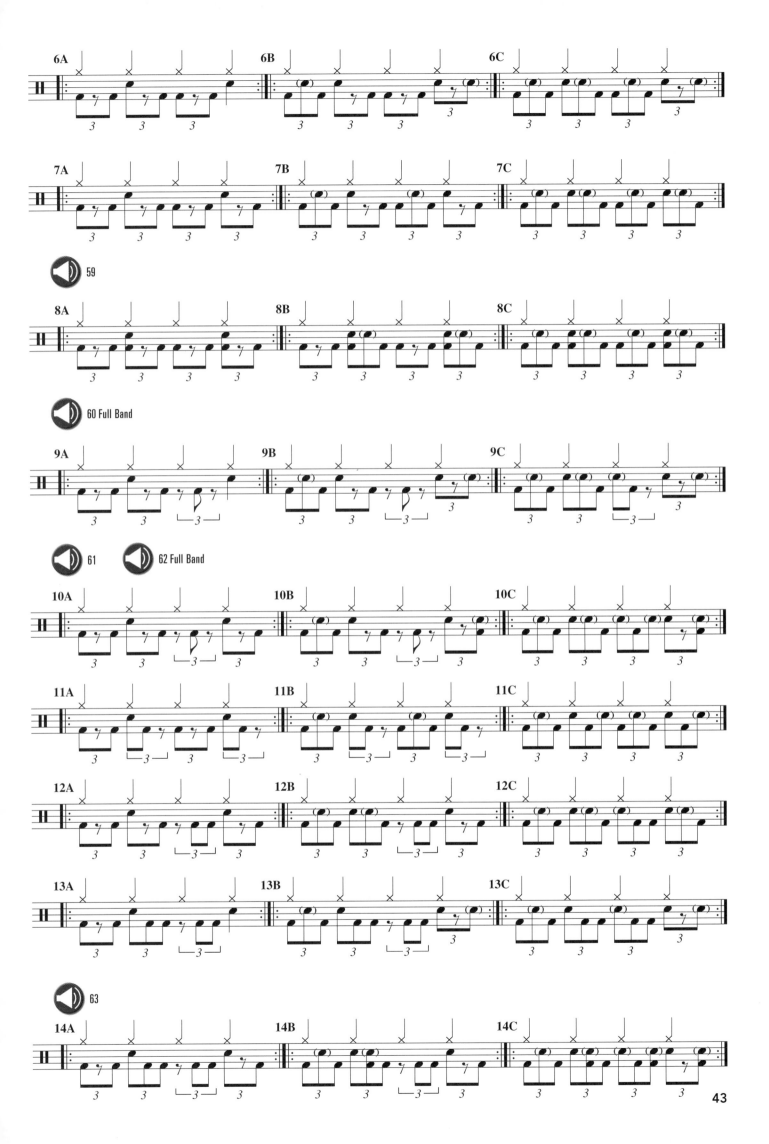

43

Triplets with Regular-Time Hi-Hat Shuffle

We will now apply the wrist rocking technique that we worked on in chapter 1 to the shuffle pattern on the hi-hat. Play the hi-hat with the shoulder of the stick on the downbeats (1, 2, 3, 4) and with the tip of the stick on the note just before the downbeat. This is also known as the blues shuffle. Here are a few examples to show how this transposition will look. You may find it easier to play this hi-hat pattern over all fourteen "A" examples, before trying "B" and "C" with the ghost notes, to get used to the new pattern with your hi-hat hand.

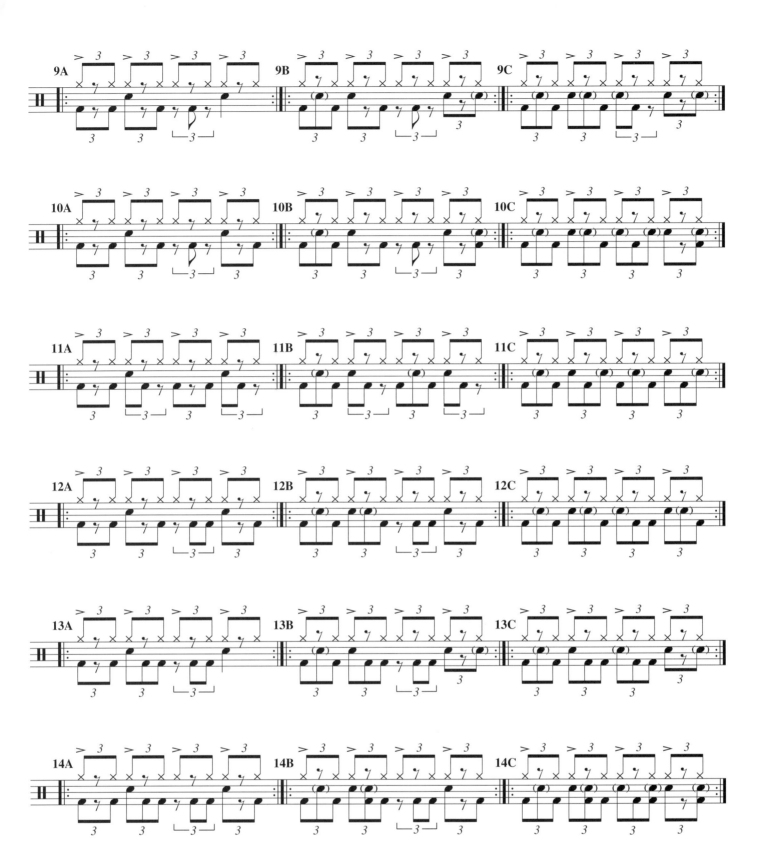

Half-Time Shuffle

The half-time shuffle is like the regular-time shuffle in the respect that it is based on triplets. The difference is that the snare accent is played on beat 3 as opposed to beats 2 and 4. This shift in the accented snare drum to beat 3 makes the beat feel as though it is cut in half, but it also gives the beat more of a laid-back kind of groove.

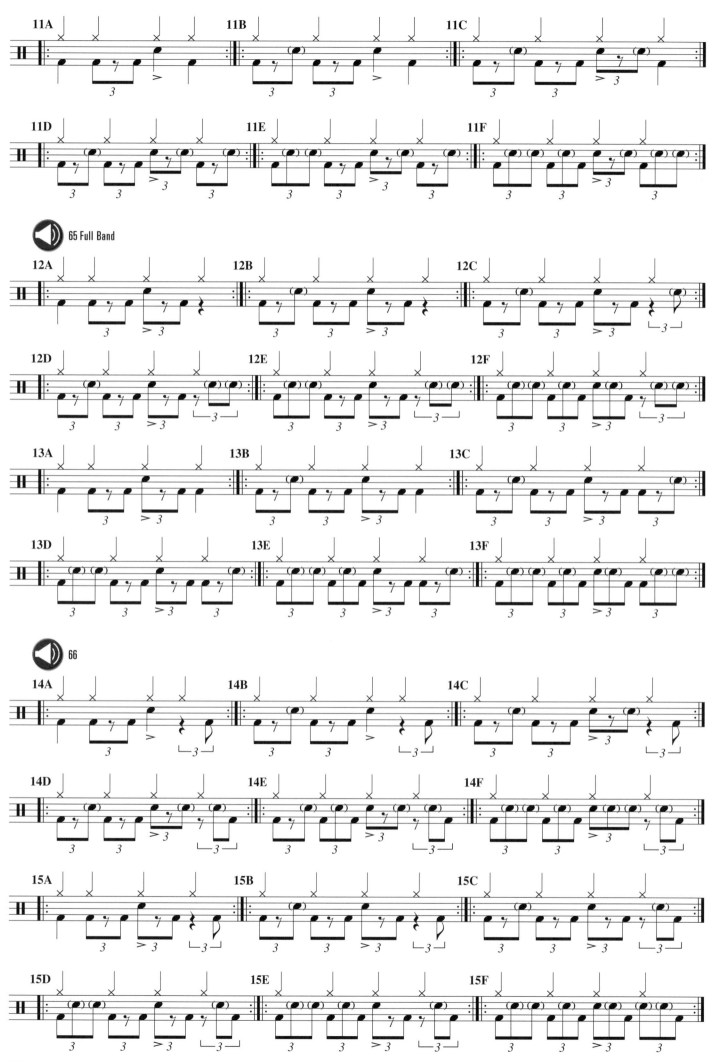

Shuffle with Wrist Rocking Technique

We will now apply the wrist rocking technique that we worked on in chapter 1 to the shuffle pattern on the hi-hat. Play the hi-hat with the shoulder of the stick on the downbeats (1, 2, 3, 4) and with the tip of the stick on the note just before the downbeat.

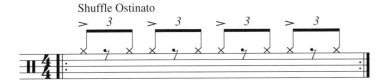

Here is an exercise to get your hands used to playing this ostinato with the half-time feel before putting it with the half-time beats.

The next step is adding the snare drum accent on beat 3.

We are going to use this pattern as our ostinato and start placing the bass drum in different locations within the measure.

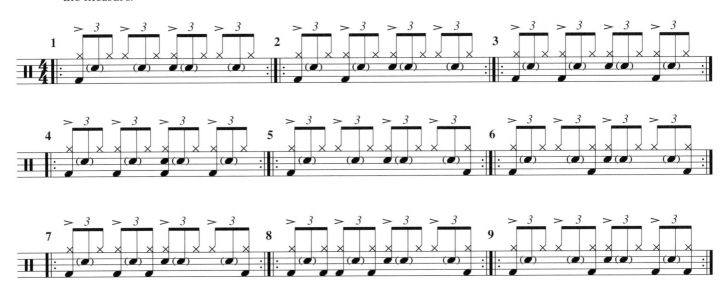

Half-Time Shuffles with Ostinato

Here are some examples combining the shuffle ostinato with some of the bass and snare patterns from the half-time exercises beginning on page 46. Try applying this ostinato to all of the exercises in the half-time shuffle section.

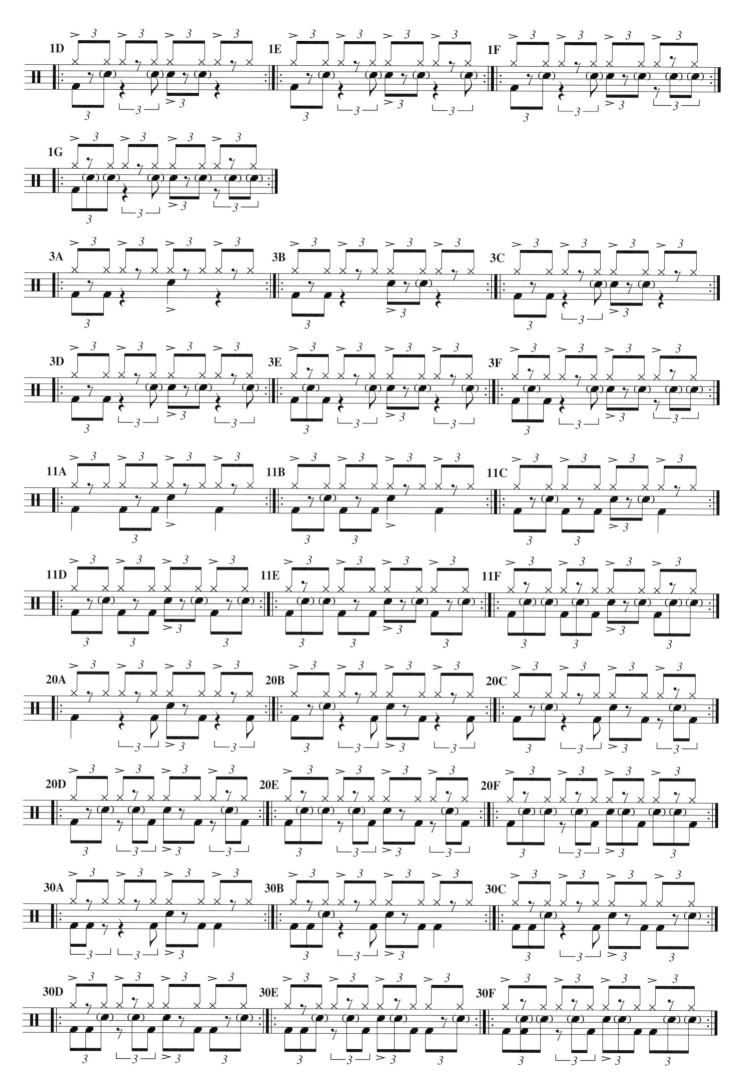

CHAPTER 6

Applying Different Hi-Hat Ostinatos

Now that you are comfortable playing the exercises in this book to an eighth-note ostinato on the hi-hat in the straight-ahead section, let's push the boundaries a bit further. These ostinatos can be played on either the hi-hat or ride cymbals. These patterns are some of the most widely used.

Hi-Hat Ostinatos

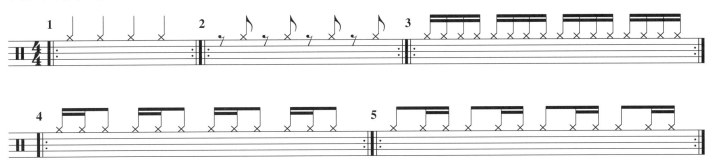

We will begin by applying the first of these ostinatos to the exercises in chapter 1. Make sure that you feel comfortable playing the ostinato that you choose to work on over all of the basic beats in chapter 1 before applying them to the later chapters. Here is each ostinato played with a few examples from chapter 1.

Ostinatos over Chapter 1

Now that you have worked through the basic exercises with whichever ostinato you chose, try to apply that ostinato to the exercises in chapters 2–4. Here are some samples.

Ostinatos over Beat 2 from Chapter 2

Ostinatos over Beat 11 from Chapter 2

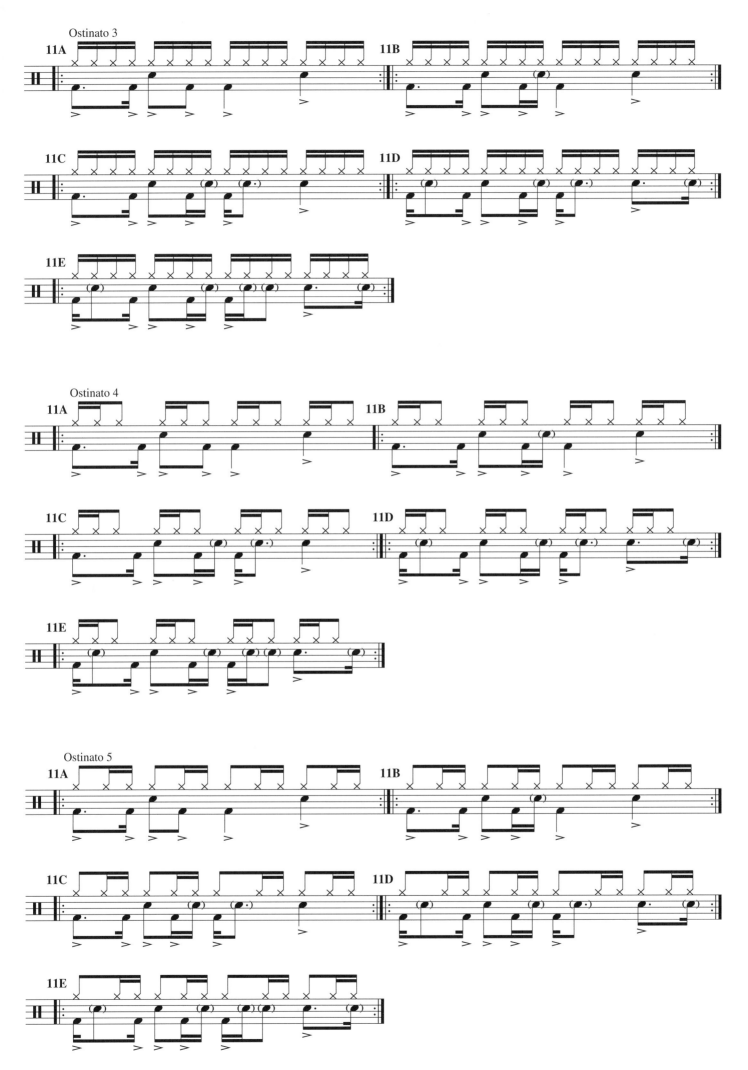

SUGGESTED LISTENING

Herbie Hancock; Harvey Mason, drummer. "Chameleon," *Head Hunters*. Columbia Records, LP KC32731 (1973).

John Mayer; Steve Jordan, drummer. "Waiting on the World to Change," *Continuum*. Columbia Records, LP 82876 79019 1 (2006).

Robert Glasper Experiment; Chris Dave, drummer. "Let It Ride," *Black Radio 2 (Deluxe Edition)*. Blue Note, LP 001866202 (2013).

Live; Chad Gracey, drummer. "Insomnia and the Hole in the Universe," *Secret Samadhi*. Radioactive, RASSD-11590 (1997).

Oz Noy; Keith Carlock, drummer. "Which Way Is Up," *Fuzzy*. Magnatude Records, MT-2314-2 (2007).

Oz Noy; Keith Carlock, drummer. "Cosmic Background," *Fuzzy*. Magnatude Records, MT-2314-2 (2007).

Oz Noy; Keith Carlock, drummer. "Ice Pick," *Fuzzy*. Magnatude Records, MTX-2317-2 (2009).

Oz Noy; Keith Carlock, drummer. "Schizophrenic," *Fuzzy*. Magnatude Records, MTX-2317-2 (2009).

Tower of Power; Dave Garibaldi, drummer. "What Is Hip," *Tower of Power*. Warner Bros. Records, LP 46 223 (1973).

Tower of Power; Dave Garibaldi, drummer. "Soul Vaccination," *Tower of Power*. Warner Bros. Records, LP 46 223 (1973).

Tower of Power; Dave Garibaldi, drummer. "Oakland Stroke," *Back to Oakland*. Warner Bros. Records, LP BS 2749 (1974).

Tower of Power; Dave Garibaldi, drummer. "Don't Change Horses," *Back to Oakland*. Warner Bros. Records, LP BS 2749 (1974).

Tower of Power; Dave Garibaldi, drummer. "Squib Cakes," *Back to Oakland*. Warner Bros. Records, LP BS 2749 (1974).

Steely Dan; Bernard Purdie, drummer. "Babylon Sisters," *Gaucho*. MCA Records, LP MCA-6102 (1980).

Toto; Jeff Porcaro, drummer. "Roseanna," *IV*. Columbia, LP FC37728 (1982).

311; Chad Sexton, drummer. "Amber," *From Chaos*. Volcano, LP 61422-32184-1 (2001).

Maroon 5; Matt Flynn, drummer. "Sunday Morning," *Songs About Jane*. J Records, LP 82365 50001 2 (2002).

Candlebox; Scott Mercado, drummer. "You," *Candlebox*. Warner Bros. Records, LP 9 45313-2 (1993).

Oasis; Alan White, drummer. "Wonderwall," *(What's the Story) Morning Glory?* Epic, EK 67351 (1995).

Oasis; Alan White, drummer. "Champagne Supernova," *(What's the Story) Morning Glory?* Epic, EK 67351 (1995).

The Smashing Pumpkins; Jimmy Chamberlin, drummer. "Tonight, Tonight," *Mellon Collie and the Infinite Sadness*. Virgin, LP 7243 8 40861 2 1(1995).

The Smashing Pumpkins; Jimmy Chamberlin, drummer. "Cherub Rock," *Siamese Dream*. Virgin, LP 0170 4 61740 1 5 (1993).

Red Hot Chili Peppers; Chad Smith, drummer. "Soul to Squeeze," *Single*. Warner Bros. Records, 9 18401-2 (1993).

Red Hot Chili Peppers; Chad Smith, drummer. "Californication," *Californication*. Warner Bros. Records, LP 9 47386-2 (1999).

Dave Matthews Band; Carter Beauford, drummer. "#41," *Crash*. RCA, LP 07863 66904-2 (1996).

Hiatus Kaiyote; Perrin Moss, drummer. "The World It Softly Lulls," *Tawk Tomahawk*. Flying Buddha, LP 88883 75262 2 (2013).

The Black Crows; Steve Gorman, drummer. "Remedy," *The Southern Harmony and Musical Companion*. Def American Records, 9 26976-2 (1992).

The Black Crows; Steve Gorman, drummer. "Thorn in My Pride," *The Southern Harmony and Musical Companion*. Def American Records, 9 26976-2 (1992).

The Black Crows; Steve Gorman, drummer. "Sometimes Salvation," *The Southern Harmony and Musical Companion*. Def American Records, 9 26976-2 (1992).

The Black Crows; Steve Gorman, drummer. "Descending," *Amorica*. Def American Records, 74321 24194 2 (1994).